FUN
WITH

SCIENCE

EXPERIMENTS FOR BOYS AND

GIRLS AGED 9 TO 99

THE ENTHUSIAST

The Enthusiast

Publisher of vintage how-to, etiquette, retro cooking and home economics, holidays and celebrations, games and puzzles, graphic design, classic children's, illustrated literature and poetry, humor and anything else that delights.

What's Your Passion?

   Enthusiast.cc

   TheEnthusiast@Enthusiast.cc

ISBN / EAN

EBook Edition   1595837531 / 9781595837530
Standard Edition   159583754X / 9781595837547

Scientists do experiments to find out exactly what happens in our surroundings. Then they collect the results to make scientific laws. The experiments in this book will help you understand some of the important laws of science. Be sure to do all the experiments so that you can see for yourself how scientific laws work.

CONTENTS

EXPERIMENTS WITH AIR

EXPERIMENTS WITH HEAT

CONTENTS

EXPERIMENTS WITH NATURAL FORCES

EXPERIMENTS WITH ELECTRICITY

EXPERIMENTS WITH WATER

CONTENTS

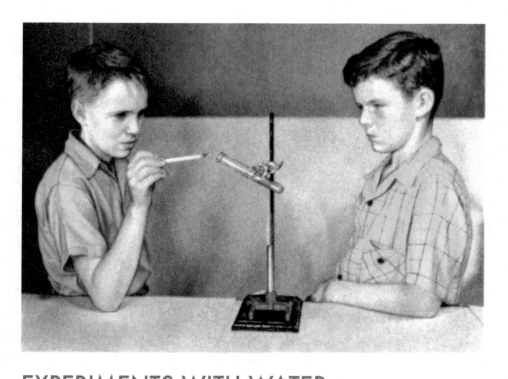

EXPERIMENTS WITH WATER (CONT.)

EXPERIMENTS WITH LIGHT

EXPERIMENTS WITH SOUND

EXPERIMENTS WITH CHEMICALS

EXPERIMENTS WITH THE HUMAN BODY

BUMPING APPLES

An Effect of Air Pressure

FOR THIS EXPERIMENT, you will need two apples and two pieces of string, each one about two feet long. Carefully tie each string around the stem of an apple. Hang the two apples from a towel rack so that they are about an inch apart If you do not have a towel rack, you can hold the two strings in your two hands so that the apples hang down, about an inch apart.

Now blow very hard between the two apples. They come together and bump!

That stream of air you blow between the two apples causes the air pressure between them to lessen. The air pressure on the outer sides of the two apples will now be stronger than the air pressure between them. This will push the two apples together and that's just what happens

You could do the same experiment using two Ping-pong balls You should use small strips of adhesive tape or Scotch tape to attach the strings to the Ping-pong halls.

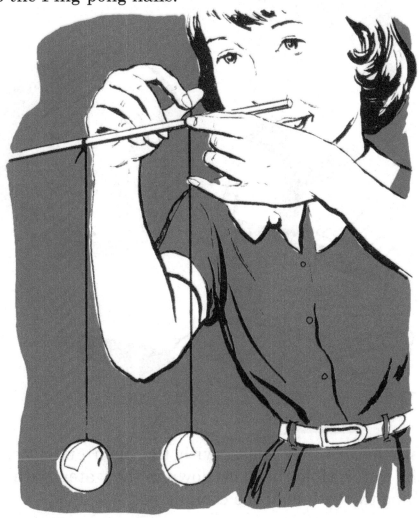

MAGIC HANDKERCHIEF

POUR WATER into a large cooking pot until it is about half-full.

Take a clean handkerchief and stuff it into an empty drinking glass. If you push the handkerchief to the bottom of the glass, it will stay there without falling out.

Now push the drinking glass, with the open end f acing down, straight into the water. Hold the glass down in the water, with the rim of the glass touching the bottom of the cooking pot.

10

Lift the glass straight out of the water. Take the handkerchief out of the glass. The handkerchief is still dry! Why? Simply because the air inside the drinking glass keeps the water from going into the glass. Two things cannot be in the same place at the same time. As long as there is air in the glass, no water can get in.

SODA STRAWS

ASK ANYONE why you can sip a soda through a straw. He'll probably answer with one word, "Suction." Then ask him what suction is. He probably won't be able to give you a good answer to that question.

Try this experiment to find out scientifically why you are able to sip a soda through a straw. Fill a glass with water or milk. Take two soda straws and sip the liquid through them.
Now take one of the straws out of the milk. Put one end of this straw in your mouth while the other end hangs outside the glass. The second straw is still dipped in the milk. Try to sip the milk through the two straws. You can't! It's impossible!

12

Why can't you sip any milk through the one straw that is still dipped in the milk?

You can only suck a liquid through a straw if you make a partial vacuum in your mouth. This means that you reduce the air pressure in your mouth.

You can reduce this pressure in your mouth by sipping. Then the air pressure on the milk in the glass just pushes the milk up into your mouth. You seem to be sucking the milk, but actually, air is pushing this milk up through the straw.

However, when one straw is hanging outside the glass, this is what happens. As you sip, you create that partial vacuum in your mouth. But the air in the hanging straw then rushes into your mouth before the milk can be pushed up into the other straw.

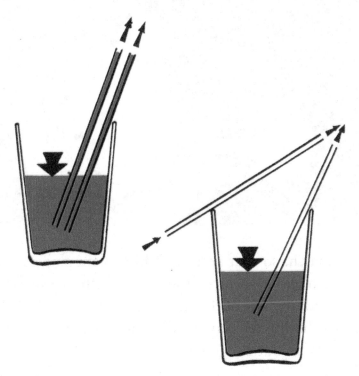

A MATCH TRICK

THIS IS another "trick." Like all tricks, there is a scientific explanation for the "magic" you see. In this case, it happens to be a very simple explanation.

Get a funnel and some matches from the kitchen. Be very careful when you use the matches. Also, make sure the funnel is clean. Put the small end of the funnel in your mouth. Strike a match and hold it about an inch away from the wide end of the funnel. Make sure that you hold the match even with the middle of the wide opening of the funnel
Blow into the funnel.

You expected the match to go out, didn't you? But instead of going out, the match flame bends toward the funnel.

Blow out the match, so that you don't burn your fingers. Then strike another match. Hold this match about an inch from the mouth of the funnel. But this time, keep the match even with the rim of the funnel.

Now blow into the funnel. Surprised? This time, the match flame bends away from you. In fact, it may go out altogether.

14

What is the explanation of this trick? When you blow into that funnel, the air you blow comes out of the funnel in a stream long the sides. This leaves very little air in the middle of the funnel,

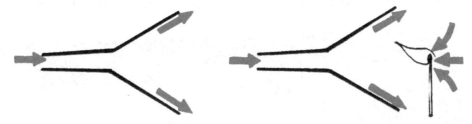

Now, when you hold the flame even with the middle of the funnel, there is very little air pressure in the middle. So the air around the match flame just, pushes it toward the middle of the funnel.

When you hold the match flame even with the tunnel, the air blows directly at the flame.. This air you are blowing out is stronger than the air around the match. That's why the flame bends away from the funnel If you blow enough, the match flame will go out.

BURNING AND RUSTING

The Importance of Oxygen

YOU MUST HAVE HEARD that when something burns, it uses up the oxygen in the air. Almost every boy and girl learns this in his science class at school. Here's a very easy way to prove it.

Light two candles and set them in your kitchen sink. Now cover one of the candles with a milk bottle. In a short time, that candle will go out, while the other one continues to burn. The candle under the bottle uses up the small amount of oxygen.
in the air of the bottle, and then the flame goes out. The other candle has all the oxygen in your room, so it will continue to burn for a long time.

Rusting of iron or steel is much like burning only it happens much more slowly than burning. Try this experiment:

Ask your mother lor a small pad of steel wool. Stuff it into the bottom of a tall drinking glass, the tallest one you can find. Set the glass upside down in a soup bowl filled with about a half-inch of water.

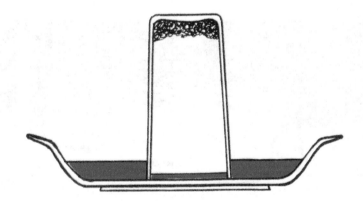

Look at the glass again the next day. You will notice that the steel wool looks rusty, and also that some of the water has risen into the glass!

What happened? The water rose in the glass. So something must have been taken out of the air in the glass to make room for the water that rose. It was oxygen that was taken out of the air. The steel wool used up the oxygen as it rusted—just as the candle used up oxygen when it burned.

HOT-AIR CANNON

Using Matches for Bullets

THIS EXPERIMENT will show you, in a very simple way, how a cannon works. You will need some wooden kitchen matches, a cork, a bottle, some string, and a candle.

Break the heads off two kitchen matches, and put them inside a thin glass bottle.

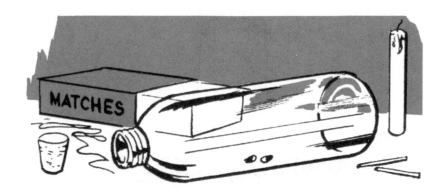

Tie two pieces of string, each about two feet long, around the bottle. Put a cork in the mouth of the bottle. Don't force it in too tightly. Now hang the bottle by the two strings from some thing like a towel rack.

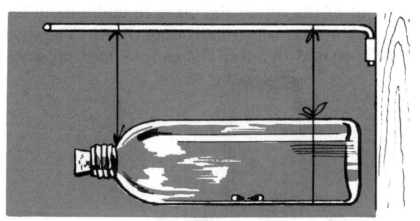

Light the candle, and then heat the bottle at a point just under the two match heads. In a minute or so, the matches will catch fire. The cork will shoot out of the bottle with a popping noise, and the bottle will "shoot" backward.

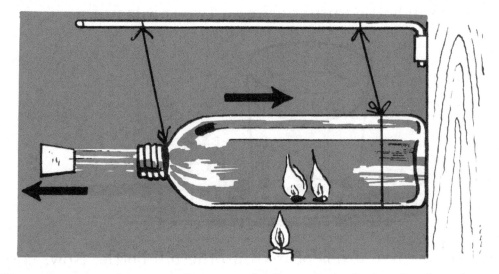

The moment the matches catch fire, the air in the bottle gets very hot. It expands and pushes out the cork with a "pop." As the cork and the hot air shoot out of the bottle, the bottle reacts by moving in the opposite direction—backward.

This is very much like a cannon and a rifle. When the gunpowder burns, the bullet shoots out, and the rifle or cannon *recoils* - that is, moves backward. Anybody who shoots a rifle must be very careful about this recoiling action. It can hurt your shoulder if you're not careful.

WEIGHING WATER

Proving That Hot Water is Lighter Than Cold

THIS EXPERIMENT will prove to you that hot water weighs less than cold water. You will need a drinking glass and a small pill bottle, plus some ink.

Fill your glass almost to the top with cold water. Then pour cold water into the pill bottle until it is about two-thirds full.

Put two or three drops of ink into the pill bottle. Now, very carefully, set the bottle in the drinking glass.

The inky water stays in the bottle. Practically no ink flows into the water in the glass.

Now empty the glass and the bottle and refill them with the same amount of water as before. But this time, put *hot* water in the pill bottle and cold water in the drinking glass. Then put a few drops of ink in the water in the bottle, as you did before. Again, stand the bottle in the glass of water.

In a few moments, the inky water will start to flow out of the bottle into the water in the glass. Soon the inky water will be spreading upward in the water.

The hot water in the bottle rises into the glass of cold water. This must mean that the hot water is lighter than the cold water. Otherwise it wouldn't rise. So you see that hot water weighs less than cold water.

A BATHTUB MOTORBOAT

Using Soap for "Gas"

HOW WOULD you like to make a small boat that moves as if it had a motor in it—and with soap as the "gasoline"? You say it can't be done! Oh, yes, it can!

Cut a very small boat, about an inch long, out of cardboard or very thin, light wood.

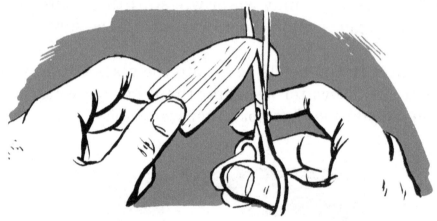

Cut a slit in the rear of your boat, and push a small piece of soap into the slit. The soap can easily be wedged into the small cut you made.

Fill your bathtub with about a foot of water. Float your boat in the water. Within a few moments, the boat will start to move forward just as if it had a motor.

What makes the boat move? It's the soap that does it. Here's how: When the boat touches the water, the soap immediately begins to dissolve. This lowers the surface tension of the water near the soap. The water at the rear of the boat no longer has the force that can hold it back. So it moves forward—and it keeps going as long as there is soap left to dissolve in the water.

HOMEMADE MAGNET

The Transference of Magnetism

IF YOU HAVE A MAGNET, you can use it to make more magnets. All you need is a piece of iron or steel—preferably steel For instance, you can make a sewing needle into a magnet. Here's how:

Hold your horseshoe magnet in your left hand and the needle in your right hand. Rub the needle along one side of the magnet.

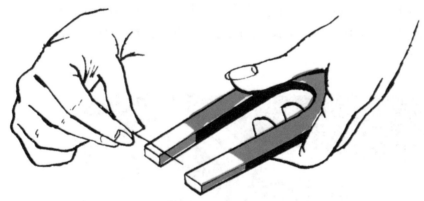

Rub the needle along the magnet twenty times. Be sure that you always rub the needle in the same direction on the magnet. Now try to pick up some very small tacks with the needle. See! The needle is now a magnet!

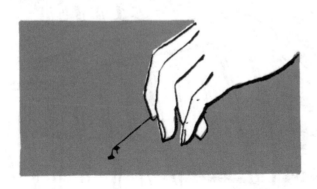

Now carefully push the needle through a thin slice of cork. You can use the cork that comes in a wine bottle. Make the slice no thicker than a quarter of an inch

If you float the cork with the needle in a dish of water, you will have a compass. Try it.

Because the needle is a magnet, it points north just as a compass does. Remember—a compass is nothing more than a magnet that is hanging, is suspended, or is floating in such a way that it can move around.

UNFRIENDLY BALLOONS

Kept Apart by Electricity

IF YOU think that all objects with static electricity attract each other, you're all wrong. Try this experiment.

Blow up two balloons and tie each one with a piece of string about two feet long. Hold the strings of the balloons, one in each hand, so that the balloons touch each other.

Now rub each balloon carefully with a piece of wool or against any clothing made of wool, like a sweater.

Hold the two balloons by their strings after you have rubbed both of them with wool. This time, as the balloons touch each other, they will bounce apart. They will push away from each other as though there were some invisible force keeping them apart.

The two balloons have become charged with electricity. When two things with the same kind of electrical charge are near each other, they push away. That's what happens to the two balloons.

If you really want to see something, try the same experiment with three balloons!

ELECTRIC SPARKS

An Example of Electrical Charges

DID YOU EVER get a shock just by touching a door handle? Did you ever get a shock just by touching your friend's hand?

Try this experiment: Walk up and down a room that has a woolen rug on the floor. Do this about ten times. Then touch your friend's hand. You will feel a shock. In fact, you may even see an electric spark where you touch her hand.

Walk across the carpet again, just as you did before, about ten times. This time, touch the doorknob instead of your friend. Again, the shock! Repeat the experiment and touch the radiator. You will see and feel the shock. You may even hear a buzzing sound for a moment.

After you touch the radiator, touch your friend again. This time, there is no spark and no shock.

Here is the explanation: When you rub your shoes on the woolen rug, you become "charged" with electricity. Then when you touch something, especially something made of metal, some bits of electricity jump from the metal to you. That's what you feel, and that's the spark you sometimes see.

But once this spark has jumped, you no longer have any electrical charge. So if you then touch your friend, you feel no shock. All the electrical charge you had is no longer there.

BOILING WITH ICE

A Question of Pressure

THEY SAY that "seeing is believing." But if you saw a piece of ice boil water, would you believe it? Try this experiment! Pour about two inches of water into a glass pot. The bottom of a glass coffee maker would be fine for this. Place the pot on your stove and heat it until the water boils. Let it boil for about two minutes.

Now put a cover on the pot and turn off the heat. Within half a minute, the water will stop boiling.

Now put a few ice cubes on the pot cover. Within a minute or two, the water will start boiling again!

It's hard to believe that the ice is causing the water to boil, but it's true. The ice cools the steam in the pot, and changes it back into water. This leaves very little steam in the pot, so the pressure of the steam on the water is very low. It is a scientific fact that when the pressure on water is very low, the water often starts to boil—even though it may not be very hot.

So it's really the low pressure on the water in the pot—rather than the ice on the cover—that makes it boil.

The experiment would work the same way if you used wet towels instead of ice. You could even use cold water instead of the ice. But make sure the glass pot you use is marked *Pyrex*.

BOBBING MOTH BALLS

An Attempt at Perpetual Motion

YOU'VE PROBABLY heard it said that it is impossible to make a perpetual-motion machine. That is a machine which would go on forever without stopping. Nobody has made one yet. But you might try this experiment to see how long you can keep something moving.

Fill a drinking glass about two-thirds full of water. Then shake about half a teaspoonful of baking soda into the water. Stir it up with the spoon until all the soda dissolves in the water.

Drop four moth balls into the water. They will sink to the bottom of the glass. Then slowly pour in vinegar until the moth bails start to move upward.

If the moth balls stop moving, add a little more vinegar. Now the moth balls will move up to the surface, then down again. They will do this again and again-up and down-for quite some time.

The explanation of this "perpetual motion" is not so simple. The vinegar and baking soda combine to produce bubbles of a gas *carbon dioxide*. The bubbles stick to the moth balls, thus making the moth balls a bit bigger, but lighter than they were without bubbles. So the moth balls rise to the surface of the water.

But as soon as they reach the surface, the bubbles of gas go Into the air. So the moth balls are now a little smaller, but heavier than they were, and so the moth balls sink. This rising and sinking will continue as long as there are vinegar and baking soda left in the glass to produce gas bubbles.

COOLING OFF

An Example of Evaporation

WHEN YOU ARE very hot on a summer day, what is the best way to cool off? A dip into the water, of course! But did you ever notice that when you come out of the water, you feel much colder than you did when you were in the water?

Is the air really colder than the water? To find out, you need a thermometer. If you have a weather-type thermometer (not the kind you take your temperature with), then you can do this experiment.

Put the thermometer in a pot of water. Hold it in the water and "read" the thermometer—that is, see what the temperature is.

Now take the thermometer out of the water and wipe it dry with a towel. Then take the temperature of the air in your room. You will see that the air is actually warmer than the water. Then why does the air feel so cold when you come out of a shower or out of the water at the beach?

You can find the answer to that question by doing another experiment.

Using absorbent cotton, rub a little alcohol on the back of your hand. Your hand feels quite cold, doesn't it?

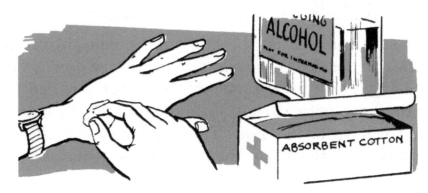

Notice that your hand gets colder and colder as the alcohol dries. Try rubbing water on the back of your hand with absorbent cotton. Your hand will get colder as the water dries.

That's just the way it is at the beach. As soon as you come out of the water, your body begins to dry. This drying makes you feel cold, just as the drying water made your hand feel cold. When alcohol dries on your body, you get even colder because it dries faster than water! This is called *evaporation*.

THE FLOATING EGG

An Example of Salt-Water Buoyancy

IF YOU lower an egg into a glass of water, the egg will fall to the bottom of the water. Try it! The egg sinks. That's no surprise to you. It's what you expect to happen.

Take the egg out of the water. Now put three small spoonfuls of salt into the water. Stir the water very well with your spoon. Then lower the egg into the salty water. This time, it will float!

Eggs float in salt water because the salt water pushes up on the egg harder than the plain water does. The salt water presses upward hard enough to hold up the egg. This upward push of the water is called buoyancy.

Maybe you have noticed that it is easier for you to swim in the salty ocean than in fresh water in a lake. That's because the salt water pushes up harder against you than the fresh water does—just as in the case of the egg!

LIGHT IN WATER

How Light Is Reflected

GO INTO A room in your house tonight where you can be in almost complete darkness. The bathroom is probably dark at night, because it usually has only one window.

Take one piece of black paper and one piece of white paper with you. If your room is totally dark, you won't be able to see either piece of paper. They will both look black. That is because you can only see something when there is light on it.

Now try this: Fill a glass with water and hold it over a lighted electric bulb. There should be no other light in your room.

Look down into the water. It is all lit up! Look at the outside of the glass. You see that it looks dark, compared with the inside.

Now put the glass on a table. Stir a piece of soap around in the water until you count off about ten seconds. This will make the water a bit cloudy.

Put the glass over the electric bulb again and look down into the water. This time, the water in the glass looks dark. Look at the outside of the glass. The outside looks lighter than the inside—just the opposite of the results in the first part of this experiment.

Here's how the scientist explains this. When you hold the clear water over the light, all the light goes through the water, but none passes through the glass. All the light is reflected from the glass into the water.

But when there is soap in the water, much of the light is reflected by the soap. This light goes outside the glass. So it looks brighter outside than it does inside.

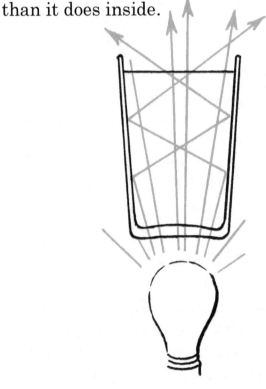
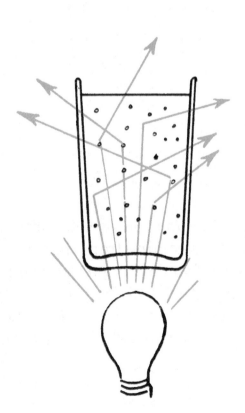

THE BROKEN PENCIL

The Effect of Bent Light

FILL A drinking glass with water almost to the top. Stand a pencil in the water and let it lean against the rim of the glass. The pencil will look as if it is broken at the rim of the glass.

Now do the same experiment with a drinking glass only half- filled with water. This time, the pencil seems to be broken at the surface of the water.

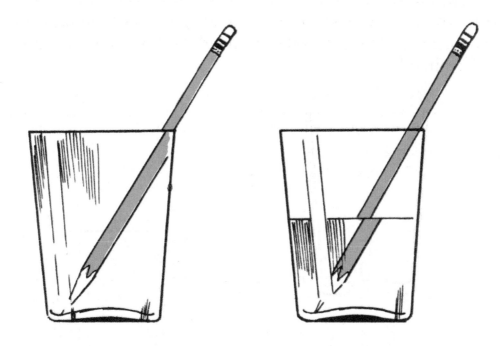

The explanation of the "broken pencil" is this: When you see the pencil, light is coming from that pencil straight to your eyes. Light comes to your eyes from every part of the pencil — the part that's in the water, and the part that's in the air. Light from the top of the pencil goes right through the air to your eyes. But the light coming from the bottom of the pencil has to go through the water and then through the air.

Whenever light goes through water and then through air, it changes its direction, or bends, slightly. So the part of the pencil in the water seems to be pointed in a slightly different direction. That's why it looks broken.

You will notice the same thing happening the next time you are in a row boat or a canoe. Look at the oar. It will appear to be broken, just as the pencil did.

NOISY PAPER

An Experiment with Sound Vibrations

SOUND is made whenever something vibrates. You can make paper vibrate by blowing on it. Try it. You really don't get much of a sound, because the paper doesn't vibrate fast enough to produce a real sound.

Now take two strips of paper about an inch wide and seven or eight inches long. Flatten them against each other. About an inch from one end, place your thumb and second finger around the paper strips and then spread the strips apart near the end.

Blow between the paper, Blow hard! You will hear a squealing sound.

The reason you hear the squeal is that your breath makes the two strips of paper vibrate very fast. This fast vibration produces a high-pitched sound.

If you can get two leaves or two blades of grass, try the same experiment. You will be surprised at the high note you can make when you blow between them.

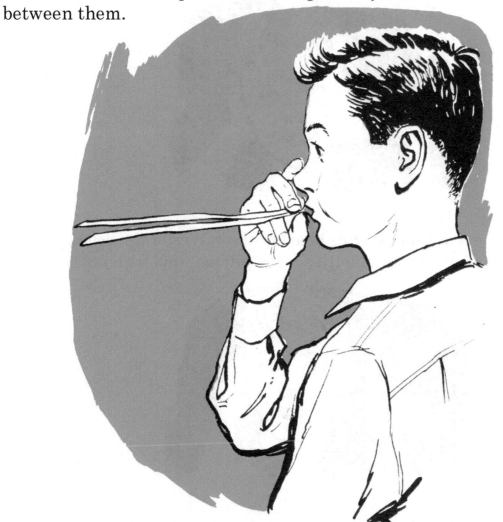

SEA SOUNDS AT HOME

An Aural Illusion

WHAT is an aural illusion? Well, you've probably heard of an optical illusion. That's when your eyes fool you into believing you see something that really isn't there. In an aural illusion, you think you bear something that isn't there.

In this experiment, you will think you hear the sounds of the sea.

Close one ear with your hand and put an empty drinking glass over the other.

Doesn't it seem that you are hearing the waves of the ocean?

Try the same experiment with a large pitcher, one with not too large an opening.

Again, you hear the sounds, but they roar even louder than they did with the glass. You can try many different objects, anything you can "cup" over your ear. In every case, you will hear the sounds of the sea.

When you next go to the seashore, try listening to the sounds of the sea in an oyster shell or a snail shell,

All the small sounds in the air around you cause the shells or the glass or the pitcher to vibrate. Then the air inside, next to your ear, starts to vibrate. Since it is so close to your ear, it sounds very loud. That's why you hear something that sounds like the roar of the sea.

THE SINGING BOTTLES

An Experiment with Air Vibrations

IF YOU SING the note "A" near a violin, the A string on the violin will begin to "sing" also. You will hear the A string as if someone were playing it very softly. If you sing the note "E" near the violin, then the E string of the violin will begin to sing.

When you sing, you make the air vibrate. And this air will make the string of the violin vibrate, but it will only affect the string that corresponds to the note you are singing. This is called *sympathetic vibration.* You can do a neat experiment with sympathetic vibration by using two bottles. The bottles must be of the same size and shape—for example, two soda bottles.

Blow across the mouth of one of the bottles. You will hear a pleasant musical note.

Blow across the mouth of the other bottle. Again, you will hear a pleasant musical note—in fact, the same sound as the first one.

Now hold one bottle to your ear while you blow across the mouth of the other bottle.

The bottle against your ear will begin to "sing" the same note that you blow across the first bottle. This is sympathetic vibration. The air vibrating in the first bottle causes the air to vibrate the same way in the other one.

Now, what do you think would happen if you used two bottles of different sizes? Try it!

The bottle against your ear doesn't sing this time. You might say that the two bottles are not "in tune" with each other, so there is no sympathetic vibration.

EAR TO THE GROUND

How Sound Travels

HAVE YOU EVER seen a picture of someone with his ear to the ground? Did you ever see a man put his ear to a rail to hear a train approaching? In both cases, they are trying to hear something that they would not be able to hear standing up.

Try these experiments, and you will understand why they can hear through the ground.

Stand near a table and have your friend tap on the other end of the table. You hear a rather soft tapping sound. Now kneel down and press your ear to the table while your friend is tapping. It now sounds very loud.

Hold a pencil near your mouth and scratch the pencil point
with your finger. You may hear a very faint sound or no sound at all. Now
hold the end of the pencil in your teeth while you scratch the point. This
time, the scratching sounds loud.

Whenever you hear something through a solid substance like the ground,
a rail, your teeth, the table, and so forth, it sounds loud. It sounds much
louder than it does when you hear it through air. This is because sounds
move more easily through solids than through air.

DISAPPEARING WINE

A Magician's Trick

DID you ever see a magician pour wine from one glass into another? He says the magic word, "Abracadabra/' and presto! The wine changes to water as he pours it.

It's not magic at all You can easily do the same thing. Here's how;

Fill a wine glass about half-full of water, and add a few drops of red ink, If you haven't got red ink, blue ink will do just as well.

Take another empty wine glass and put a few drops of a bleach into it. Your mother has some around the house. Ask her if you can use some.

The glass with just a few drops of bleach will look empty to anyone else but you. Now show the "trick*' to a friend or your sister or brother.

Simply say, "Abracadabra, as you pour the "wine* into the "empty" glass. The "wine" will become "water" as it falls into the glass.

How can you explain the mysterious change in color from red to no color at all? Easy!

The bleach turns the red ink into a colorless liquid. It works the same way as it does when your mother uses bleach to whiten clothing that she is washing. The red ink and the bleach react to produce a new chemical substance—a colorless one!

A GAS CANNON

Using Carbon Dioxide to Create Pressure

THIS EXPERIMENT should be done outdoors—just in case!

The cannon you will make is a soda pop bottle with a cork that fits tightly. You will make the gas that fires the cannon out of vinegar and baking soda. If your mother doesn't these things, you can get them at the grocery store at very little cost.

Here's what to do: Pour about an ounce of vinegar into your bottle. An ounce will take up about a half-inch in your bottle. Now put a tea-spoonful of baking soda into a small square of tissue paper. Roll up the paper into a little package.

Now take everything outside the house. Then put the paper package in the bottle and place the cork in the mouth of the bottle. The cork should be neither too tight nor too loose—just about right.

In a few moments, the mixture will begin to fizz in the soda bottle. Step away from the bottle and wait. After a short while, the cork will be shot out of the bottle with a loud "pop"!

What happens is this: The vinegar and the baking soda mix together and combine. They form bubbles of a gas called carbon dioxide. This gas builds up pressure in the bottle until it finally shoots our the cork.

OIL AND WATER

How Soap Acts As a Cleaning Agent

WHEN YOUR mother tells you to wash your hands before dinner, she means: *Get the dirt off your hands!* Do you use plain water or soapy water' Soapy water, to be sure!

But why does soap wash dirt away better than plain water? What is there in the soap that does this job so well? Try this experiment in order to find the answer.

Pour water into a drinking glass until it is about half-full Then put in about a tablespoonful of any cooking or salad oil. What happens? The drops of oil float to the top of the water and come together into one big drop of oil.

Stir the oil with the spoon, and you will see the oil breaking up into tiny drops. But within ten or fifteen seconds after you stop stirring, all the drops will float to the surface again.

Now add a little soap powder or ordinary soap. Stir the water with a spoon. The oil will break Into thousands of tiny drops and spread through the water. But this time, when you stop stirring, the drops will not come together at the surface. They will remain spread throughout the water.

The soap causes the oil to break into thousands of tiny drops which stay separate from each other. These drops can easily be washed away. The bits of dirt that stick to the tiny drops are carried away with the soapy water.

Scientists use the word *emulsify* to mean the breaking up of an oil into small drops. Soaps emulsify many kinds of oil, and that's why soap can clean!

ACID OR ALKALI

Using Red Cabbage as Litmus Paper

IF YOU have a chemistry set, you have probably noticed strips of *litmus paper* in it. This is a special paper that you use to discover whether a material is an acid or an alkali. If you do not own a chemistry set, you can make something like litmus paper out of red cabbage leaves.

Tear up two leaves of red cabbage into small pieces Put them into a bowl or a pot (not an aluminum one) and add about a cup of boiling water.

Let the cabbage water stand until it turns purple This may take as long as an hour Now it is ready to be used as an acid alkali tester

Pour a little vinegar (an acid) into a drinking glass, and add some of the cabbage water. In a few moments, the mixture will change from purple to red. This is the test for an acid—a red color with cabbage juice.

Now pour some ammonia (an alkali) into another glass. Your mother probably has some ammonia around the house. It is used as a cleaning liquid.

Add a few drops of the cabbage juice to the ammonia in the glass. This time, the purple cabbage juice will turn green. This change to a green color is the test for an alkali.

You can test many liquids around the house to find out whether they are acids or alkalis. Just mix a little bit of the liquid with a little bit of die cabbage juice. If the mixture turns red, then it's an acid. If it turns green, it's an alkali.

YOUR PULSE

WHEN YOU GO to your doctor's office for an examination, about the first thing he does is to take your pulse. He wants to find out it it's fast or slow, and if it's strong or weak.

You can find out some things about yourself by taking your pulse. Here's how to do it. Put the second and third fingers of your right hand on your left arm, just above the wrist.

You may have to move your fingers around a bit to find the pulse. You'll feel it bump up and down against your two fingers. Use a watch with a second hand, and count the number of pulse beats in one minute.

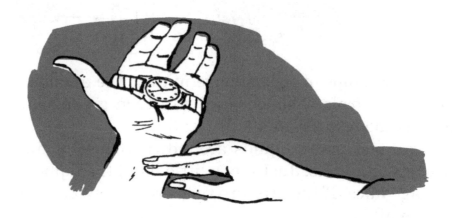

Do some exercise, like running or bending and stretching, for about a minute or two. Immediately time your pulse again. It will be much faster and stronger than before.

Take the pulse of everyone in your family. You will find that each person's pulse beats at a different rate.

You can also take your pulse by pressing your second, third, and fourth fingers into the flesh of your neck, just under your chin, but about two inches to the left.

HOMEMADE MOVIES

Finding out How Pictures Move

HERE IS THE experiment that gave scientists the idea for inventing movies. All you need for this is two small index cards, a pencil, and a rubber band.

Draw a line across the width of one card so that you just about divide the card in half. Then, on one half of the card, draw a picture of a fish bowl.

Divide your second card in half, just as you did with the first one. On the upper half of the second card, draw the same fish bowl—but draw it very lightly, so that you an easily erase it later. Then draw two or three goldfish in the bowl. These should be drawn with a dark pencil or crayon.

Now erase the fish bowl The bowl was drawn just so you could put the goldfish in the right place on the card.

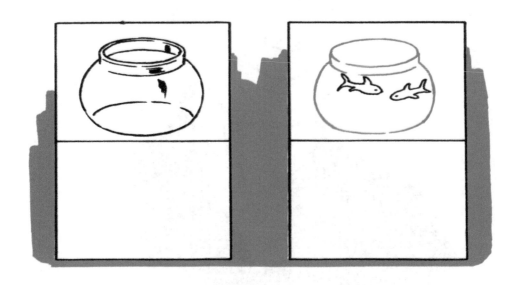

Turn the second card upside down and put the two cards
back to back, so that the picture of the bowl is on one side, and the picture
of the fish is on the other side at the other end. Slip your pencil over one
of the cards and hold it in position by twisting the rubber band around it.

Hold the ends of the pencil between your fingers and twirl the pencil very fast. As the cards twirl, the goldfish will appear to be inside the bowl.

Your eyes hold a picture for an instant after it has actually gone.
When you twirl the cards rapidly, the pictures follow each other so fast
that you see both pictures at the same time.

When you watch movies, the pictures go so fast that you see "movement," although you are really seeing many still pictures, one after the
other.

THE PHANTOM FINGER

The Effect of Double Images

HERE IS A simple experiment which you can do in about five seconds. And you need nothing for it except your two eyes and your two hands.

Touch the second fingers of your two hands together and hold them about six inches in front of your eyes. What do you see? Exactly what you'd expect to see—two fingers touching each other.

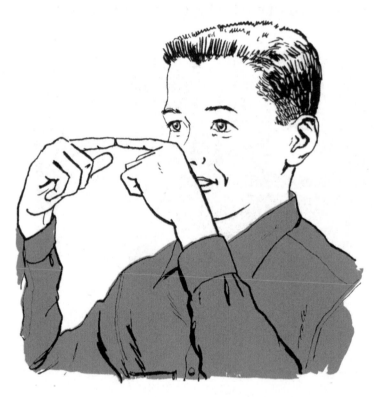

Now look past your fingertips at the wall in your room. Out of the corner of your eyes, you will see "the phantom finger" between your two fingers. The odd part of this is that the finger will appear to have two fingernails!

The extra finger, of course, is not really there. Each of your two eyes sees both fingers. When these images overlap, you seem to have three fingers—and the middle one has two fingernails.

CPSIA information can be obtained
at www.ICGtesting.com
Printed in the USA
LVOW05s0543141217
559682LV00016B/1041/P